First Facts®

Long Ago and Today

# SCHOOL
## LONG AGO and TODAY

by Sally Lee

**Consultant:**
Daniel Zielske
Professor of Anthropology
South Central College
North Mankato, Minnesota

WITHDRAWN

**CAPSTONE PRESS**
a capstone imprint

First Facts are published by Capstone Press,
1710 Roe Crest Drive, North Mankato, Minnesota 56003
www.capstonepub.com

**Library of Congress Cataloging-in-Publication Data**
Lee, Sally.
School long ago and today / Sally Lee.
pages cm.—(Long ago and today)
 Includes bibliographical references and index.
ISBN 978-1-4914-0296-2 (library binding)
ISBN 978-1-4914-0304-4 (paperback)
ISBN 978-1-4914-0300-6 (ebook PDF)
1.  Education—United States—History—Juvenile literature. 2.  Schools—United
States—Juvenile literature. I. Title.
LA205.L38 2015
370.97309—dc23
                              2013050325

**Editorial Credits**
Nate LeBoutillier, editor; Juliette Peters, designer; Eric Gohl, media researcher; Tori Abraham,
production specialist

**Photo Credits**
Capstone Studio: Karon Dubke, 21; Corbis: Bettmann, 9, National Geographic Society/George
King, 7; Library of Congress: 4, 11, 15; Shutterstock: chippix, cover (top), Ermolaev Alexander,
background, Everett Collection, 5, 13, Monkey Business Images, cover (bottom), Nucleartist, 1
(right), Pressmaster, 17, Timolina, 1 (left), Tyler Olson, 18.

Printed in the United States of America in North Mankato, Minnesota
032014      008087CGF14

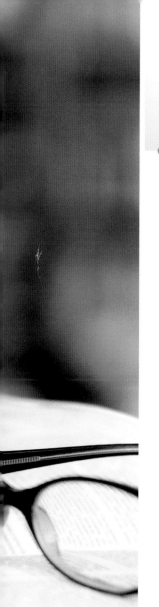

# TABLE OF CONTENTS

# BIG CHANGES

America's first schools might seem dull to children today. Early schools had few books or other supplies. Only a few subjects were taught. As life in America changed, so did schools. Today preschoolers learn a lot from TV, computers, and adults before they reach kindergarten. Schools then introduce new subjects and learning styles.

5

# TEACHING AMERICAN INDIAN CHILDREN

American Indians lived in North America long before white European settlers came. They didn't have schools. Children learned the skills they needed from adults. Men took boys hunting and fishing. Girls helped women cook and make clothes. Older **tribe** members told children stories about their tribe's history and beliefs.

**tribe**—a group of people who share the same ancestors, customs, and laws

an Alaskan Indian
family in 1917

# SCHOOLS
## IN THE 13 COLONIES

**Colonial** schools in the early 1700s had one room and one teacher. Children wrote with chalk on slates because there wasn't much paper. They spoke their lessons out loud. Young children learned to read from **hornbooks**. Older children studied the *New England Primer,* a book that taught children to read. Many lessons also came from the Bible.

**colonial**—having to do with the 13 British colonies that became the United States

**hornbook**—a paddle-shaped board covered with a sheet of paper and a thin layer of cow's horn

New England colonial school

# PIONEER SCHOOLS

Families began moving westward in the 1850s. **Pioneer** children had many chores at home. Schools were closed during spring planting and fall **harvesting**. Many children walked as far as 3 miles (4.8 kilometers) to their one-room school. One teacher taught all grades. Some schools couldn't afford books. Children brought any books they had at home.

**pioneer**—a person who is among the first to settle a new land
**harvest**—to gather crops that are ripe

ASH GROVE
DIST    45.

schoolhouse in
Oklahoma in 1916

# SCHOOLS
## IN THE EARLY 1900S

City schools in the United States were crowded in the early 1900s. Many children were **immigrants**. They had to learn English in school. When the United States joined World War I (1914–1918) in 1917, American kids learned about the countries fighting in the wars. They collected scrap metal and rubber. These materials were used to make weapons.

**FACT:**
Some children didn't go to school in the early 1900s. Many worked on farms or in factories. Others sold newspapers.

**immigrant**—a person who leaves one country and settles in another

# SCHOOLS
## IN THE 1950S AND 1960S

**Integration** was a challenge for U.S. schools in the 1950s and 1960s. In some places African-American children were not allowed to go to school with white children. People fought to change this for many years. Now most schools are for children of all races.

**integration**—the end of the separation of races

Washington, D.C., integrated school in 1955

# SCHOOLS TODAY

**Technology** has changed schools. Now kids use the Internet to **research**. They use computers to read, write, and create projects. Computers can also help with science, math, music, and other subjects. Many schools have large computer screens the whole class can see.

**FACT:**
A 2011 study by an American Internet company showed that more children aged 2 to 5 years knew how to play a computer game than ride a bike.

**technology**—the use of science to do things

**research**—to study and learn about a subject

# SCHOOLS IN THE FUTURE

Future schools will use more technology. Computers will come in different forms. Even now some computers are small enough to wear like watches, eyeglasses, or jewelry. Others are as big as trucks and function with touch screens. There is no telling what shapes and forms technology in schools will take.

# TIMELINE

| SCHOOL EVENTS | | WORLD EVENTS |
|---|---|---|
| | **2500 BC** | Great Pyramids built in ancient Egypt |
| First *New England Primer* is printed and used to teach reading and life skills in colonial schools | **AD 937** | England becomes a nation |
| | **1690** | |
| The first of the *McGuffey Readers* is printed and will be used in schools for the next 100 years | **1775–1783** | American Revolutionary War |
| | **1836** | |
| First American Indian school opens in Pennsylvania | **1861-1865** | American Civil War |
| | **1879** | |
| First school air raid drills held in United States because of Soviet Cold War threat | **1914–1918** | World War I |
| | **1939–1945** | World War II |
| | **1945** | |
| The U.S. Supreme Court rules that separate schools based on race are unlawful | **1950s** | Start of human space exploration |
| | **1954** | |
| The Civil Rights Act helps integrate U.S. schools | **1964** | |
| First computers are used in schools | **1969** | Man lands on the moon |
| First home computers appear | **1977** | |
| Internet rises to popular usage | **1990s** | Hubble Space Telescope launched into space |
| Apple puts out its first iPad, which quickly moves into schools | **2010** | |

## The Schoolchildren's Blizzard

In 1888 a surprise **blizzard** hit the Midwest while children were at school. Strong winds ripped the roof off a one-room school in Mira Valley, Nebraska. Minnie Freeman had to get her 16 students to safety. But the blowing snow outside made it impossible to see. Getting lost could mean freezing to death. Miss Freeman kept the children close together. She led them safely to her home.

**blizzard**—a heavy snowstorm with strong wind

# Hands On:
## MAKE A HORNBOOK

**What You Need:**
pen or markers
thin cardboard
paper
scissors
glue or tape
clear plastic wrap

Colonial children used hornbooks to learn the alphabet, numbers, and Bible verses. Hornbooks were made from wood, paper, and a thin layer of cow's horn. You can make your own from everyday things found at home.

**What You Do:**
1. Draw the shape of a paddle on cardboard. The top should be a bit bigger than your piece of paper.
2. Cut out the paddle.
3. Write the alphabet in capital letters on the piece of paper. Then write the letters in lowercase.
4. Glue or tape the paper onto the paddle. Trim paper if needed to be sure it fits the paddle.
5. Carefully cover the paper with plastic wrap. Fold it neatly over the edge of the paddle. Tape the plastic wrap to the back.

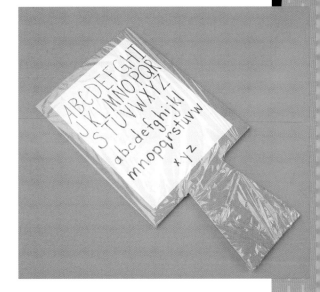

# GLOSSARY

**blizzard** (BLIZ-urd)—a heavy snowstorm with strong wind

**colonial** (kuh-LOH-nee-uhl)—having to do with the 13 British colonies that became the United States

**harvest** (HAR-vist)—to gather crops that are ripe

**hornbook** (HORN-buk)—a paddle-shaped board covered with a sheet of paper and a thin layer of cow's horn

**immigrant** (IM-uh-gruhnt)—a person who leaves one country and settles in another

**integration** (in-tuh-GRAY-shuhn)—the end of the separation of races

**pioneer** (pye-uh-NEER)—a person who is among the first to settle a new land

**research** (REE-surch)—to study and learn about a subject

**technology** (tek-NOL-uh-jee)—the use of science to do things

**tribe** (TRIBE)—a group of people who share the same ancestors, customs, and laws

# READ MORE

**Hinman, Bonnie**. *The Scoop on School and Work in Colonial America*. Life in the American Colonies. Mankato, Minn.: Capstone Press, 2012.

**Pelleschi, Andrea**. *The Life of a Colonial Schoolteacher*. Jr. Graphic Colonial America. New York: Powerkids Press, 2014.

**Shelton, Paula Young.** *Child of the Civil Rights Movement*. New York: Schwartz & Wade Books, 2010.

# INTERNET SITES

FactHound offers a safe, fun way to find Internet sites related to this book. All of the sites on FactHound have been researched by our staff.

Here's all you do:

Visit *www.facthound.com*

Type in this code: 9781491402962

Super-cool stuff!

Check out projects, games and lots more at
**www.capstonekids.com**

## CRITICAL THINKING USING THE COMMON CORE

1. Why do you think people came up with the idea of having schools? (Integration of Knowledge and Ideas)

2. Look at the picture on page 11 and read the text on page 10. In what ways have school buildings changed since the days of pioneer schools? (Integration of Knowledge and Ideas)

## INDEX